IT'S MY STATE!

COLORADO

Linda Jacobs Altman

Stephanie Fitzgerald

Marshall Cavendish
Benchmark
New York

Library of Congress Cataloging-in-Publication Data
Altman, Linda Jacobs, 1943-
       Colorado / Linda Jacobs Altman, Stephanie Fitzgerald. — 2nd ed.
          p. cm. — (It's my state!)
       Summary: Surveys the history, geography, government, and economy of
       Colorado as well as the diverse ways of life of its people.
       Includes index.
       ISBN 978-1-60870-046-2
        1. Colorado—Juvenile literature. I. Fitzgerald, Stephanie. II. Title.
  F776.3.A45 2011
  978.8—dc22   2010003903

Second Edition developed for Marshall Cavendish Benchmark by RJF Publishing LLC (www.RJFpublishing.com)
Series Designer, Second Edition: Tammy West/Westgraphix LLC
Editor, Second Edition: Amanda Hudson

All maps, illustrations, and graphics © Marshall Cavendish Corporation. Maps and artwork on pages 6, 24, 25, 76 and back cover by Christopher Santoro. Map and graphics on pages 9 and 41 by Westgraphix LLC.

The photographs in this book are used by permission and through the courtesy of:
Front cover: Fraser Hall/Getty Images and Brian Bailey/Getty Images (inset).
Alamy: blickwinkel, 4; Jill Stephenson, 10; Dennis Flaherty, 11; imagebroker, 12; Corbis RF, 13; Chris Howes/Wild Places Photography, 14; Stock Connection Distribution, 15; Alexey Stiop, 20; CameraShots – Travel, 22; Hind Sight Media, 38; MARKA, 40; David W. Hamilton, 42; Blaine Harrington III, 47; Blend Images, 50; Jack Affleck, 60; Caroline Commins, 70; Zach Holmes, 74. (17). **AP Images:** David Zalubowski, 52; Bryan Kelsen, 53. (2). **Colorado.gov:** 43; 57. (2). **Colorado Historical Society:** Charles S. Stobie, 23. (1). **Colorado State University:** Plowing on the College Farm, Colorado State University, University Alumni Photograph Collection, Archives and Special Collections, 33. (1). **Denver Public Library; Western History Collection:** E. Jump/X-11485, 30; Louis Charl McClure/MCC-4295, 34; Harry Mellon Rhoads/Rh-5794, 35. (3). **Getty Images:** Wolfgang Kaehler, 5 (top); Joel Sartore/National Geographic, 5 (bottom); John E Marriott, 16; James Gritz, 17 (top); Laurie Campbell, 17 (bottom); Greg Probst, 18 (top); Stephen Oachs Photography, 18 (bottom); Gail Shumway, 19; MPI/Stringer Hulton Archives, 31, 32; AFP, 36, 45 (bottom); Jeff Christensen, 44; Mark Wilson, 45 (top); John E Moore, 46; John Kelly, 48; George Rose, 54; MICHAEL GOTTSCHALK/AFP, 59; Kevin Moloney/Stringer, 62; Leanna Rathkelly, 63; George Rose, 65; John Moore, 66; Bloomberg, 68 (top); Richard Cummins, 68 (bottom); John Moore, 69. (25). **Library of Congress:** Rep#LC-USZ62-55218, 27. (1). **Photolibrary:** Table Mesa Prod./Index Stock Imagery RF, 49. (1).

Printed in Malaysia (T).
135642

COLORADO

CONTENTS

THE CENTENNIAL STATE

A Quick Look at
COLORADO

State Flower: Rocky Mountain Columbine

This small and delicate columbine grows in the rugged Rocky Mountains. Edwin James discovered it in 1820, when he led the first successful climb of Pikes Peak. On April 4, 1899, the Rocky Mountain columbine became the official state flower.

State Bird: Lark Bunting

The perky little lark bunting is native to Colorado's eastern grasslands. It arrives each year in springtime and flies south in September. The males have a spectacular mating song of warbles and trills.

State Tree: Colorado Blue Spruce

The majestic blue spruce is named for its silvery blue color. A truly giant specimen can be found in Colorado's Gunnison National Forest. It is more than 126 feet (38 meters) high and measures 5 feet (1.5 m) around the trunk.

State Fossil: Stegosaurus

Colorado's state fossil is the plant-eating dinosaur Stegosaurus. The Denver Museum of Nature and Science displays one of the most complete skeletons ever found. The bones of this plate-backed dinosaur were discovered in 1937 by a group of high school students and their teacher during a field trip.

State Insect: Colorado Hairstreak Butterfly

The hairstreak butterfly became Colorado's official insect on April 17, 1996. This tiny, brightly colored butterfly adds a flash of beauty to the Colorado mountainside.

State Animal: Rocky Mountain Bighorn Sheep

The Rocky Mountain Bighorn Sheep became Colorado's official state animal on May 1, 1961. The male bighorn stands about 3 feet (1 m) at the shoulder and may weigh as much as 300 pounds (136 kilograms). Its magnificent curving horns make it instantly identifiable.

COLORADO

Dinosaur National Monument

Craig

Yampa River

Grand Lake

Lake Granby

Boulder

Pawnee National Grassland

Sterling

South Platte River

Greeley

Yuma

Colorado River

Vail

Denver

Grand Junction

Aspen

Leadville

Pikes Peak

Colorado National Monument

Mount Elbert

Sawatch Range

Gunnison

Continental Divide

Colorado Springs

Big Sandy River

Gunnison National Forest

Pueblo

Arkansas River

John Martin Reservoir

Telluride

Rio Grande

Alamosa

Sangre de Cristo Mountains

La Junta

Canyons of the Ancients National Monument

San Juan Mountains

Durango

Comanche National Grassland

Trinidad

Mesa Verde National Park

N
W E
S

The Centennial State

Colorado is a place of contrasts. The state is made up of sixty-four counties, which include rugged western landscapes, soaring mountain ranges, and flat grassland prairies. With an average elevation of 6,800 feet (2,100 kilometers) above sea level, Colorado is the highest state in the nation.

The state is commonly divided into four geographical regions: the Eastern Plains, the Front Range—or the Piedmont, as it is sometimes called—the Rocky Mountains, and the Colorado Plateau. Each of these regions has its own special features.

The Eastern Plains

The Eastern Plains of Colorado are part of the Great Plains region of the central United States. This vast grassland prairie is flat and dry. It is subject to howling winds and long periods of drought, or lack of water. The land is used for farming and raising livestock.

Rainfall averages 15 to 20 inches (38 to 51 centimeters) per year, but

Quick Facts

COLORADO BORDERS

North	Wyoming
	Nebraska
South	New Mexico
	Oklahoma
East	Nebraska
	Kansas
West	Utah

it comes in spurts. Weeks of dryness can be followed by days of rain and hail. Eastern Colorado farmers use both irrigation and dryland farming methods to make their land productive.

Like most farming areas, eastern Colorado is not heavily populated. It is a place of farms and small towns, with an average of about five people per square mile.

The Front Range

The Front Range stands between the Eastern Plains and the western mountains. It is about 50 miles (80 km) wide and 275 miles (445 km) long. Its elevation ranges from 4,921 to 14,110 feet (1,500 to 4,300 m) above sea level. The terrain is rugged, with many different land forms. There are cone-shaped "tepee buttes" and mesas with flat tops and steep sides. The mysterious and beautiful Garden of the Gods is located just west of Colorado Springs. Still farther west, on the edge of the Front Range of the Rocky Mountains, lies Pikes Peak.

The red sandstone formations in the Garden of the Gods were formed by erosion. Over long ages, wind and water carved the soft stone into fantastic shapes that look like ordinary objects. Famous landmarks include elephant rock (you can even see its trunk!), balanced rock, and sleeping giant. When two surveyors came upon the area in 1859, they were struck by its beauty. One of them mentioned that it was "a fit place for the gods to assemble." The man, Rufus Cable, named the spot Garden of the Gods.

Two formations at the entry to the garden frame a large purple mountain in the distance. That is Pikes Peak, standing like a guard at the edge of the Rocky Mountains. At 14,110 feet (4,300 m) above sea level, Pikes Peak is the thirty-first-highest peak in Colorado. It is the most visited mountain in North America. Two hundred years ago, pioneers in their wagon trains saw it and knew they had reached their goal.

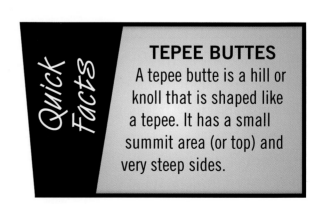

Quick Facts

TEPEE BUTTES
A tepee butte is a hill or knoll that is shaped like a tepee. It has a small summit area (or top) and very steep sides.

Colorado Counties

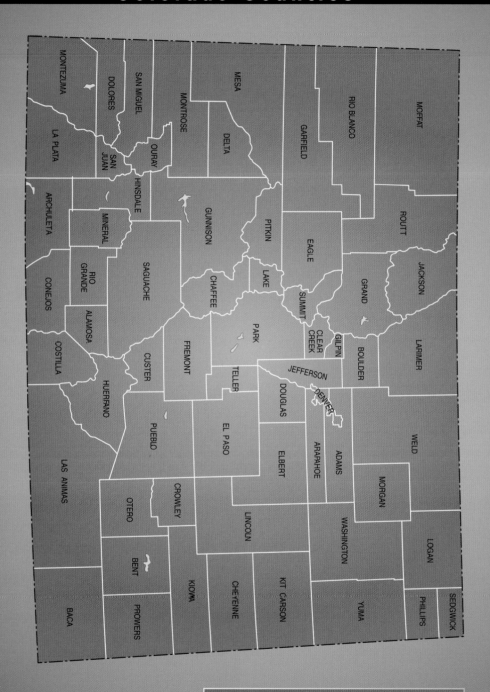

Colorado has 64 counties.

The sandstone shapes in the Garden of the Gods were formed by erosion.

Pikes Peak was named for Zebulon Pike. In 1806, he was the first American explorer to see it, but he never reached the top. He set out to climb the peak but was forced back by a blizzard. Edwin James made the first successful climb in recorded history in 1820.

Many pioneers never made it beyond Pikes Peak and into the Rockies. They settled in the Front Range instead, drawn by the cool climate, fresh mountain air, and beautiful surroundings.

Today, about 80 percent of Colorado's people live in this region. The state's largest cities—Denver, Colorado Springs, Aurora, and Lakewood—are there. Denver, the state capital, is the largest city in Colorado. It is nicknamed "the mile-high city" because its elevation is 5,280 feet (1,610 m)—exactly one mile above sea level.

The Rocky Mountains

The Rocky Mountains are called the backbone of North America because the Continental Divide runs through them. Rivers east of the divide flow toward the Atlantic Ocean and Gulf of Mexico. Rivers to the west of the divide flow toward the Pacific. The Rockies are not a single mountain range but a group of more than one hundred individual ranges. They run a distance of approximately 3,000 miles

There are more than one hundred mountain ranges in the Rocky Mountains.

(4,800 km). The Rockies stretch from northern Alberta, Canada, all the way down into New Mexico.

The Colorado Rockies are grouped into two large "belts" running north and south through the center of the state. The belts are separated by a series of high mountain valleys. At least 1,000 peaks in the Colorado Rockies are more than 10,000 feet (3,000 m) above sea level. Fifty-four are over 14,000 feet (4,300 m) high. Almost no one lives in the upper reaches of those fifty-four mountains. Even the bighorn sheep leave in winter, seeking lower—and warmer—territory.

The Rockies as a whole are sparsely populated, averaging only two people per square mile. The population is concentrated in the high mountain valleys, where

The Colorado Plateau, in the western part of the state, is not heavily populated.

level ground makes farming and ranching possible. There are no major cities in the Colorado Rockies, but there are a number of thriving small towns.

Two of the best-known of Colorado's mountain towns are Aspen and Leadville. Both began as silver mining towns and were almost destroyed when the mining boom ended. However, both survived, and they have grown into very popular resort towns.

The Colorado Plateau

The Colorado Plateau is a truly western landscape. It is a place of mountains and mesas, valleys and canyons. Along the western slope of the Rockies are woodlands of juniper and piñon pine. Farther west, trees give way to semidesert shrub lands.

Colorado is known for its fresh air and beautiful surroundings.

Like the high mountains and the eastern plain, western Colorado is thinly populated. Its largest city is Grand Junction, with about 42,000 people. Orchards and vineyards dominate the landscape around Grand Junction. With irrigation, western Colorado provides ideal conditions for wine grapes. Peaches, cherries, and nectarines are also grown there.

Three famous sites in western Colorado are Mesa Verde National Park, Four Corners National Monument, and Dinosaur National Monument. At Mesa Verde—Spanish for "green table"—ancient cliff dwellings seem to grow out of the rock. The structures were created by a people known today as the Ancestral Pueblo people. The park has more than four thousand archaeological sites

Rock art created by the Fremont Indians can be found at Dinosaur National Monument.

containing the remains of ancient human habitation. The remains date back to 600 CE.

The Four Corners National Monument is the only place in the country where a person can be in four different states at the same time. The monument is located on the Navajo Indian Reservation at the point where Arizona, Colorado, New Mexico, and Utah meet.

Dinosaur National Monument is one of the largest dinosaur fossil sites in the world. Earl Douglass, a paleontologist (a scientist who studies prehistoric life), found the quarry in 1909. Over the years, the quarry has yielded thousands of bones, including many nearly complete skeletons. The site also contains rock art—petroglyphs and pictographs—made by the Fremont Indians who lived in the area 800 to 1,200 years ago.

Rivers and Lakes

The biggest lakes in Colorado are reservoirs, which were created by damming the flow of mountain streams. Blue Mesa Reservoir is the largest of these artificial lakes, covering about 29 square miles (75 square km). There are dozens of natural lakes in the mountains. The largest of them, Grand Lake, covers about one square mile.

Colorado is the birthplace of four major rivers. The Colorado River begins west of the Continental Divide. It flows southwest for 1,470 miles

Grand Lake is the largest natural lake in Colorado.

(2,370 km) to the Sea of Cortez. The Rio Grande is located east of the Divide, as are the South Platte River, which flows into the Missouri, and the Arkansas River, which flows into the Mississippi.

Climate

On Colorado's Eastern Plains, summers are hot, winters are cold, and rainfall is scarce. In central and western Colorado, altitude determines the type of weather and average temperature. For example, the winter temperature in the high mountain city of Leadville averages 24 degrees Fahrenheit (-4 degrees Celsius). The plains town of Colorado Springs averages about 31 °F (-0.6 °C). In July, differences are even more pronounced, with Leadville averaging 53 °F (12 °C) and Colorado Springs 68 °F (20 °C).

Annual snowfall also shows how climate is related to elevation in Colorado. Leadville can receive more than 200 inches (508 cm) of snow a year, while Colorado Springs gets around 42 inches (107 cm). A Rocky Mountain blizzard is something to behold. For example, in 1990, a single storm dropped 50 inches (127 cm) of snow at Echo Lake in north-central Colorado. Wind-driven snow brought traffic to a stop on the highway between Boulder and Denver. After the storm, work crews had to clear snowdrifts 12 feet (4 m) high before they could reopen the road.

One of Colorado's strangest weather patterns is the chinook wind. The chinook winds are warm and dry, swooping down from the mountains at near-hurricane speeds. They can raise the temperature forty or fifty degrees Fahrenheit in an hour's time.

In Their Own Words

Leadville has ten months of winter and two months of late fall.

—John Henry "Doc" Holliday, famous outlaw

Wildlife

From the plains to the plateau, Colorado's wildlife is varied and interesting. The Eastern Plains have small mammals such as rabbits, prairie dogs, skunks, and ground squirrels, along with the coyotes that feed on them.

Wherever there are prairie dogs, there will be burrowing owls. These small brown owls live in abandoned

Burrowing owls are a threatened species.

Mountain lions are rare, but they can be found in Colorado.

prairie dog burrows. Burrowing owls are on Colorado's list of threatened species. Their habitat is shrinking, partly because development is destroying prairie dog towns. Colorado's Partners in Flight program has created a conservation plan. It includes protecting burrows and reducing the use of insecticides, especially during the owls' breeding season.

Colorado's mountains are home to elk, moose, and bighorn sheep. Foxes, badgers, and beavers also thrive in the region. Bears may also be found, but only a few of these creatures live year-round at the highest altitudes. Like the bighorn sheep, some of these bears move to lower altitudes for winter.

The animals of western Colorado have at least one trait in common. All can survive in a land of little rainfall. Porcupines, weasels, hares, and mule deer live where the juniper and piñon pine give way to sand and sagebrush. Predators that hunt these animals include coyotes, bobcats, and mountain lions. Golden eagles may also be found in this area.

A golden eagle looks similar to a large hawk.

Plants & Animals

Aspen

The Aspen is Colorado's only widespread, native deciduous tree. It is most commonly found in the western two-thirds of the state. The tree has a grayish-white trunk and green leaves that turn a beautiful yellow-gold color in mid-September.

Moose

Colorado's moose live in some of the state's forests and are most often found in North Park. An adult moose can weigh more than 1,000 pounds (455 kg). Moose have long legs that are good for walking through deep snow. They eat mainly plant material such as leaves, berries, and grasses.

Lynx

This large cat has grayish-brown fur and tufts of hair at the tops of its ears. By 1973, it seemed as if the lynx might have disappeared from Colorado. A restoration program was started in 1999. The program was successful. By 2005, more than two hundred lynxes had been released into the wild, and a number of litters had been born.

Bald Eagle

Two decades ago, bald eagles were extremely rare in the lower forty-eight states. Thanks to conservation efforts in Colorado, however, the state had more than a hundred breeding pairs in 2008, and sightings have become increasingly common. These majestic birds live high up in the trees, near reservoirs or other large waterways. They feed on fish and small mammals.

Porcupine

Sharp-quilled porcupines are plant-eaters that feast on berries, flowers, leaves, and other parts of trees. Porcupines cannot throw their quills, but the sharp spines are an effective defense against predators.

Juniper

Different types of juniper grow across the state. These evergreen shrubs produce red berries that provide food for Colorado's wildlife. Humans, however, should never eat these berries. They can be poisonous.

From the Beginning

Colorado's first people, known as Paleo-Indians, arrived about 13,000 years ago. They hunted mastodons, mammoths, and other gigantic creatures. When big game became scarce, the Paleo-Indians turned to hunting smaller game. They also began gathering plant matter to supplement their diets.

The descendants of these early people were also hunter-gatherers. The descendants used to be called Anasazi, which is a Navajo word meaning "enemies of our ancestors." Today, the preferred term is Ancestral Pueblo people. From 500 BCE to about 800 CE, these ancient peoples were known as Basket Makers, because they made beautiful baskets that had many uses. The next phase of the people's history, 800 CE until about 1300 CE, was known as the Puebloan era. During this time, the Ancestral Pueblo people built magnificent homes into the cliff faces of southwestern Colorado and farmed the land above. Some of these homes are still standing today. Other native peoples, including the Ute, Comanche, Cheyenne, Arapaho, and Kiowa, also made their homes in what is now Colorado. They lived undisturbed by outsiders until the first Spanish explorers arrived in the early sixteenth century.

These explorers were followed in time by settlers who came for the land, and fortune seekers who came for the silver and gold. All played a part in the often stormy history of the Centennial State.

The Ancestral Pueblo people built homes into the cliffs of Colorado.

Beautifully preserved American Indian remains and artifacts can be seen in Mesa Verde National Park.

The Earliest Settlers

The Ancestral Pueblo people have long been a mystery to archaeologists. Exactly who were they? How did they learn to build magnificent, multistory "apartment houses"? Why did they suddenly abandon it all and seemingly disappear? Nobody knows all the answers to these questions. What scientists and historians do know is that the Ancestral Pueblo people were hunters and gatherers. They also made pottery and developed farming techniques. The Ancestral Pueblo people built their homes using sandstone rocks held together with adobe (sun-dried clay and straw). Many of these homes are extraordinary cliff dwellings. The remains of these magnificent structures can still be seen in Mesa Verde National Park.

No one knows for certain why the Ancestral Pueblo people seem to have disappeared. Some scholars blame a long drought that destroyed the crops. Many think that the Ancestral Pueblo people migrated out of the area to join other native cultures. The Pueblo, an American Indian group found in the Southwest, are the descendants of the Ancestral Pueblo people.

The Ute often moved their camps as they hunted large prey. Their tepees were easy to put up and take down.

Long after the Ancestral Pueblo people were gone, other American Indian peoples continued to settle in what is now Colorado. These included the Cheyenne, Kiowa, Arapaho, Comanche, and Ute. Most of these natives were hunters and gatherers. They often followed the buffalo herds on the Eastern Plains, bringing along their homes and families.

The Ute favored higher altitudes. Some of them lived 10,000 feet (3,050 m) above sea level. For food they gathered wild plants and fished in the rivers and streams. They also hunted elk and deer, using the meat for food and using the hides for their homes and clothing. Later, the Ute traded the hides and other goods for horses and other necessities. The Ute were skilled riders and used horses for hunting. But life for all the American Indian groups in the region began to change as European explorers and settlers arrived in greater numbers.

Quick Facts

MESA VERDE NATIONAL PARK

Mesa Verde National Park is home to four thousand archaeological sites, including the remains of ancient pit houses and cliff dwellings. The Cliff Palace, which contains more than 150 rooms in which people lived—plus storage areas and ceremonial rooms—is the largest cliff dwelling in North America.

MAKING ANCESTRAL PUEBLOAN SANDALS

Hundreds of years ago, the Ancestral Pueblo people wove sandals from yucca plants. You can copy their sandal design using cardboard, thin cord, and yarn. But unlike the Ancestral Pueblo people's, your sandals will not be sturdy or weatherproof—so you should wear them only indoors.

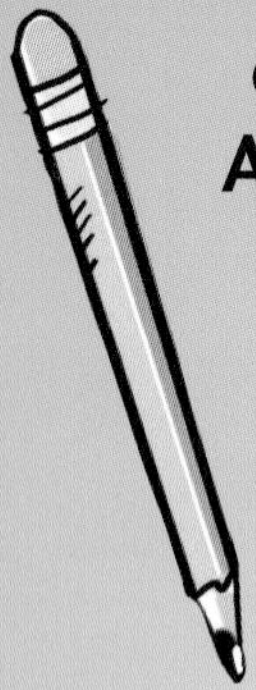

WHAT YOU NEED

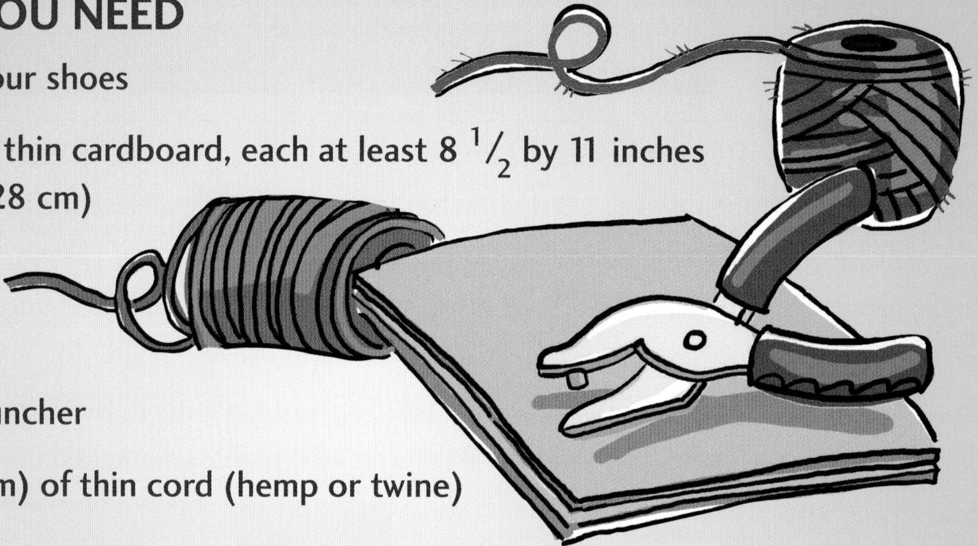

A pair of your shoes

2 pieces of thin cardboard, each at least 8 $\frac{1}{2}$ by 11 inches (22 by 28 cm)

A pencil

Scissors

A 1-hole puncher

12 feet (4 m) of thin cord (hemp or twine)

A ruler

11 feet (3.5 m) of yellow or brown yarn

Put one shoe on a piece of cardboard. Trace around it. Cut out the tracing. Write "toe" near the toe end. Mark six dots, evenly spaced, along one edge. Start at least an inch (2.5 cm) from the toe, and stop at least 2 inches (5 cm) from the heel. Make the dots about 2/3 inch (2 cm) from the edge. Mark six dots along the other edge. Each dot should be directly across from a dot on the other side. Punch a hole at each dot. Make sure the cord slides easily through each hole.

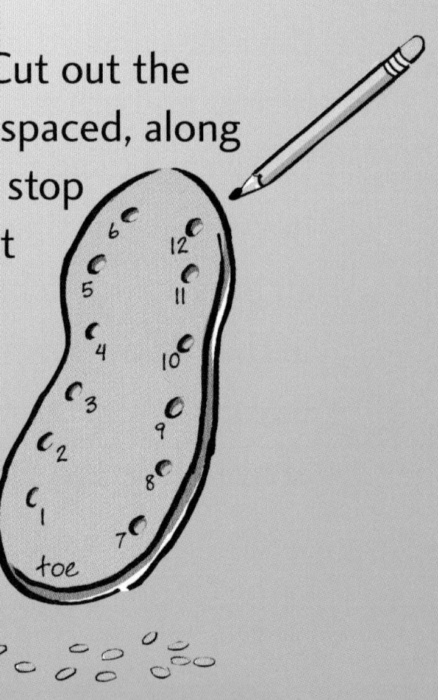

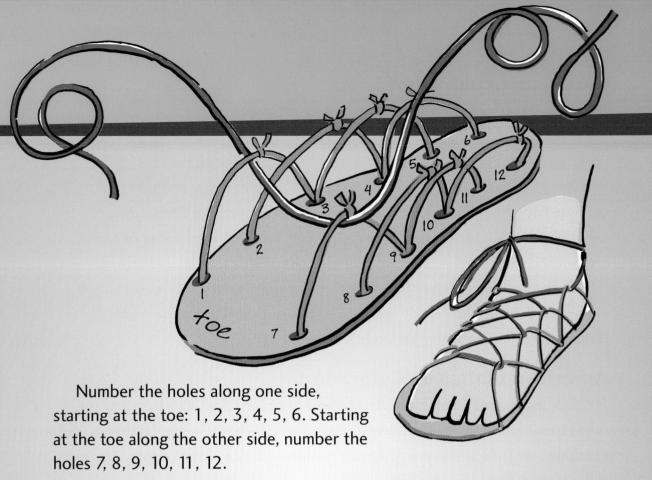

Number the holes along one side, starting at the toe: 1, 2, 3, 4, 5, 6. Starting at the toe along the other side, number the holes 7, 8, 9, 10, 11, 12.

Cut 16 pieces of cord, each 8 inches (20 cm) long.

Slide a piece of cord into hole 1 and out of hole 3. Tie it into a loop with a strong knot.

Tie another piece of cord in a loop through holes 2 and 4. Do the same with holes 3 and 5; 4 and 6; 7 and 9; 8 and 10; 9 and 11; and 10 and 12.

Pull the yarn through the two loops closest to the toe, one on each side. Center the yarn so that it is the same length on both sides.

Slide your foot (without a sock) into the sandal.

Cross the ends of the yarn on top of your foot. Pull each end through the next loop moving toward your heel. Cross the ends of the yarn again. Lace them through the next pair of loops. Continue crossing and lacing until you have used all of the loops. Pull the yarn ends behind your ankle, cross them, and tie them in front. Repeat these steps for the second sandal, and you will have a complete pair.

European Exploration

In 1682, a French explorer named René-Robert Cavelier, sieur de La Salle, claimed a huge area of land in central North America for France. La Salle himself never visited the region that is now Colorado; he simply claimed everything between the Mississippi River and the Rocky Mountains. The territory extended northward to the present-day Canadian border and south to the Gulf of Mexico. La Salle named this vast region "Louisiana" in honor of King Louis XIV of France.

The Spanish were the first Europeans to actually explore Colorado. In 1706, Juan de Ulibarri led an expedition as far as present-day Pueblo. He promptly claimed the "new" territory for Spain.

American Claims on Colorado

In 1803, the United States bought the whole Louisiana Territory from France for $15 million. With one purchase—which became known as the Louisiana Purchase—President Thomas Jefferson doubled the size of the country. The next step was to explore this new addition.

That job fell, in part, to a twenty-six-year-old army lieutenant named Zebulon Pike. In 1806, Pike set out to explore the southwestern borders of the Louisiana Purchase. It was on this trip that he discovered the peak that bears his name. Pike also had a secret mission. Spain had conquered and settled all of Mexico and most of the present-day American Southwest, including part of Colorado. The U.S. government asked Pike to check the strength of Spanish settlements in the region. Pike investigated the situation, traveling south from Colorado to the area that now includes New Mexico. He and his men were arrested by Spanish authorities and taken to Santa Fe, New Mexico, but they were later released by the Spanish.

Because of the Pike incident, the United States and Spain held talks about the boundaries of the Louisiana Purchase. In 1819, a treaty between the two nations gave northern and eastern Colorado to the United States, and southern and western Colorado to Spain.

In 1821, Mexico won its independence from Spain. It acquired all the Spanish territory in what is now the United States, including parts of Colorado. The new Mexican government did not have the resources to develop this large area, so it welcomed Americans into the Rocky Mountain wilderness.

The Mountain Men

A group of sturdy adventurers who became known as mountain men gladly accepted the invitation. They were strong, hearty men who lived by trapping beaver and other fur-bearing animals. The pelts were sold to make clothing and other goods.

The mountain men came from all over the United States and Canada. Some were interested in exploring, and some just hoped to make a profit from this

This photo shows two men setting a bear trap. Animal pelts were sold to make clothing and other goods.

new land. Many of them had little or no education, but they were wise in the ways of nature. They often served as guides, trackers, and scouts.

The mountain men knew that the American Indians still controlled the land in Colorado, and for the most part, they respected the Indians' rights. White settlement was limited to a few trading posts or forts. Both mountain men and Indians traded at these outposts. One of the best-known posts was Bent's Fort in southeastern Colorado, near the present-day town of La Junta. The legendary tracker Kit Carson once worked there. His title was chief hunter, and his job was to keep the fort well supplied with meat.

In the 1840s, the world of the mountain men began to change. Because of overtrapping, beaver populations had shrunk. Changes in fashion also made beaver fur less popular. Without as many beaver and with a smaller demand for the pelts, making a living as a trapper became very hard. This issue, combined with disaster and disease, caused the abandonment of Bent's Fort in 1849.

After the United States defeated Mexico in the Mexican-American War, which lasted from 1846 to 1848, Mexico gave up almost all of its territory in the American Southwest to the United States for $15 million. Besides part of Colorado, the territory included all of present-day California, Nevada, and Utah, and parts of Arizona, New Mexico, and Wyoming. In 1853, an additional U.S. purchase of almost 30,000 square miles (77,700 square km) of land in what is now southern Arizona and New Mexico would give the continental United States (excluding Alaska) its present borders.

"Pikes Peak or Bust!"

In January 1848, gold was discovered in California, starting one of the largest human migrations in history. During the "gold rush," about 500,000 people hoping to strike it rich headed for California. Many of these people passed through Colorado on their quest for gold. In 1858, a party led by miner William Green Russell found gold at Dry Creek, just south of the present-day site of Denver. This brought more prospectors to the area and was followed by three larger finds in Colorado in 1859. Thousands of people tacked "Pikes Peak or Bust" signs on their wagons and headed west to make their fortunes. Towns sprang up almost overnight. Montana City, Denver City, and Auraria became the core of modern Denver.

Through the 1860s, miners struck gold in different parts of Colorado. In 1860, gold was found in Leadville, one of Colorado's famous mining towns. In 1875, prospectors found a large deposit of lead carbonite ore there. The ore contained large quantities of silver. It was only the first of many silver discoveries in the area. By 1878, the city of Leadville had become one of the most important mining camps in the nation. It produced a crop of overnight millionaires.

The most famous of these mining millionaires was Horace Tabor, the Silver King. Tabor went from storekeeper to millionaire in 1877 when he "grubstaked" two prospectors, or gave them tools and supplies in exchange for a share of anything they found at the Little Pittsburgh Mine. What they found was silver—lots of it. Tabor grubstaked several other expeditions, and his fortune

In Their Own Words

One [looks] eagerly westward for a sight of the Rocky Mountains. . . . First, the highest peaks, each white with snow, loom into view, and then one after another of the great, blue-hued shoulders of the range is seen. . . . [The Rockies] do not impress one at first as being mountains; they are more like islands, with the prairie as the ocean.

—A settler describing the first sight of the Rocky Mountains

This sketch shows the booming city of Leadville in the early 1880s.

grew. In late 1879, he bought the Matchless Mine for $117,000. People thought he was crazy because the Matchless had plunged its previous owners into debt and returned nothing. But Tabor had a hunch, and he was right. By the spring of 1880, the Matchless was producing a $2,000 profit each day. Tabor became the richest of all the silver millionaires.

The good times in Leadville ended in 1893, when a severe economic depression hit the country. The government stopped buying silver to make coins. The price of silver dropped. Tabor and many other miners lost nearly everything.

Colorado Territory

The mining boom was just under way when Colorado became a U.S. territory. The status became official on February 28, 1861. The new territory immediately created a legislature, or lawmaking body, called the Territorial Assembly. At its

Quick Facts

(IN)FAMOUS FACES

Several of the Old West's most notorious killers—and famous lawmen—could be found in Leadville in the 1880s. Onetime sheriffs Wyatt Earp and Bat Masterson were there, as were outlaws Jesse James and the Younger Gang. Famous gunslinger "Doc" Holliday even had his last shoot-out in Leadville.

first meeting, the assembly created seventeen counties, made plans for a university, and chose Colorado City as the territorial capitol.

The influx of settlers became of increasing concern to American Indians in the area. In 1851, ten years before Colorado became a territory, the United States signed the Great Horse Creek Treaty with the Cheyenne. The treaty stated that prospectors and settlers would not be

**ATTENTION!
INDIAN
FIGHTERS**

Having been authorized by the Governor to raise a Company of 100 day

U. S. VOL CAVALRY!

For immediate service against hostile Indians. I call upon all who wish to engage in such service to call at my office and enroll their names immediately.

Pay and Rations the same as other U. S. Volunteer Cavalry.

...s furnishing their own horses will receive 40c per day, and rations for the same, ...the service.
...mpany will also be entitled to all horses and other plunder taken from the Indians.

...ce first door East of Recorder's Office.
HAL SAYR.

...tral City, Aug. 13, '64.

This poster from 1864 asked for volunteers to fight against American Indians.

Quick Facts

COLORADO IN THE CIVIL WAR

Colorado became a U.S. territory just weeks before the start of the Civil War (1861–1865). Its citizens were divided about which side they supported. Some sided with the Confederacy, the eleven Southern states, all of which allowed slavery, that seceded, or left, the United States after Abraham Lincoln was elected president. Other Coloradans sided with the Union (the North), which went to war to bring the Southern states back into the country. Many people in the North opposed slavery. Officially, the Colorado Territory was behind the Union cause. Nearly four thousand men served as volunteers with the Union forces. After the Union won the war, slavery was abolished throughout the United States.

This illustration shows armed soldiers in Colorado in 1852, a year after the Great Horse Creek Treaty was signed. The relationship between settlers and American Indians was tense for many years.

allowed to encroach upon the Cheyenne's traditional hunting grounds. By 1861, however, the newcomers were building houses, establishing towns, and stringing telegraph wires across the mountains and the prairies—right in the middle of the Cheyenne's land. Soldiers shot a Cheyenne chief in 1864, and the Indians responded with violence.

Then, Colorado soldiers attacked and destroyed a village in Sand Creek. They brutally murdered hundreds of Cheyenne and Arapaho, many fleeing for their lives. The Sand Creek Massacre, as it was later called, would lead to changes in federal Indian policies.

Fighting between settlers and Indians continued. The government forced many Cheyenne, Sioux, Arapaho,

In Their Own Words

Nothing lives long, except the earth and the mountains.

—Death Song of Cheyenne chief White Antelope, killed in the Sand Creek Massacre

and Ute to move off their lands and onto reservations. Nathan C. Meeker, the federal agent in charge of the Ute reservation, tried to force the Ute to become farmers. In 1879, they rebelled, killing Meeker and others. The Meeker Massacre was the last big clash between Colorado's Indians and settlers. Army forces overpowered the Indians, who returned to the reservations.

Into a New Century

On August 1, 1876, Colorado became the thirty-eighth state to join the United States. The Leadville silver boom was already under way. Hopes ran high as Coloradans settled down to the business of building a state. More schools and universities were opened. Miles of new railroad tracks were laid down. Farmers developed dryland farming techniques on the plains. Dryland farming includes, among other things, planting drought-resistant crops, as well as increasing the water absorption and reducing the moisture loss from soil. By the turn of the twentieth century, Colorado had a population of 539,700 people. Mining and agriculture were important to the economy.

As Colorado's population grew, farmers began to develop more advanced farming methods.

This photo shows the coal-mining town of Hastings around 1914, a few years before the town suffered a devastating coal-mine fire.

Colorado's mining industry survived the silver collapse of 1893, largely because of gold. A few gold strikes kept the industry going. Some mines also made money from coal and other minerals.

Farmers on the Eastern Plains used a combination of dryland farming methods and irrigation to develop the land. They produced good crops of sugar beets, as well as wheat and other grains.

When World War I (1914–1918) began, Great Britain and its allies in Europe needed raw materials. They bought food products from Colorado farms and metals such as tungsten and molybdenum from Colorado mines. When the United States entered the war in 1917, Colorado farmers and miners increased production even more.

During the 1920s, Colorado built paved highways for automobile traffic and expanded its oil industry. By 1930, the state's population topped one million for the first time in history.

Also by 1930, the American stock market had collapsed and so had the economy of the nation. This began what came to be known as the Great Depression. In Colorado as elsewhere, many people lost their jobs and some lost their homes. The economy did not recover until the United States entered World War II in December 1941. The U.S. government decided that Colorado would be a safe location for military installations and other federal facilities. Soon, a number of government offices, defense plants, and military bases were located in the state. Many of them stayed after the war ended, and so did the people who staffed them. President Dwight D. Eisenhower established the U.S. Air Force

Three girls stand in the snow in Denver during the Great Depression. In the Depression, some people lost their homes and had to live in what were known as tent cities.

The U.S. Air Force Academy, located in Colorado Springs, was established in 1954.

Academy in 1954. Four years later, the Colorado Springs facility was ready to admit students.

By 1960, Colorado's population had grown to more than 1.7 million. Three counties in the Front Range—Denver, Adams, and Jefferson—grew especially rapidly. The state's Eastern Plains lost people as quickly as the Front Range gained them. During the 1970s and 1980s, the suburbs around Denver became more heavily populated.

Throughout the 1980s and 1990s—and into the twenty-first century—the old standbys of mining and agriculture became less important to Colorado's economy. Old mining towns such as Aspen and Telluride found new life as expensive ski resorts. Technological industries flourished, and tourism became an important source of income for the state.

Important Dates

★ **800 CE to 1300 CE** The culture of the Ancestral Pueblo people flourishes.

★ **1682** La Salle claims a vast territory, which includes Colorado, for France.

★ **1706** Spaniard Juan de Ulibarri explores part of Colorado.

★ **1803** The United States buys land, including part of Colorado, from France in the Louisiana Purchase.

★ **1806** Zebulon Pike discovers Pikes Peak.

★ **1848** Mexico cedes the remainder of Colorado to the United States.

★ **1858** Gold is found at Dry Creek, near present-day Denver.

★ **1861** The U.S. Territory of Colorado is officially established.

★ **1864** During the Sand Creek Massacre, nearly 300 American Indians are killed by the Colorado militia.

★ **1876** Colorado becomes the thirty-eighth U.S. state.

★ **1878** The Leadville silver boom begins.

★ **1879** Ute and American soldiers fight during the Meeker Massacre, the last big battle between American Indians and settlers in Colorado.

★ **1914** World War I begins in Europe, and Colorado supplies raw materials.

★ **1941** The United States enters World War II. Military and government installations are built in Colorado.

★ **1958** The U.S. Air Force Academy, near Colorado Springs, opens.

★ **1960s** The skiing and tourism industries grow.

★ **1995** Denver's state-of-the-art international airport opens.

★ **1998** Quarterback John Elway leads the Denver Broncos to the first of two straight Super Bowl wins.

★ **2001** Invesco Field at Mile High, a $364-million football stadium, opens in Denver.

★ **2008** The Democratic National Convention is held in Denver. Barack Obama, the first African-American president of the United States, is officially nominated there.

The People

In a state historically known for prospectors, trappers, and hardy pioneers, more than 80 percent of Coloradans now live in cities. Many families still live in rural communities or on farms, but the cities and suburbs draw the most residents.

The Denver-Boulder-Greeley metropolitan area alone has about 2.6 million people. That is more than half the entire population of the state. City living has not destroyed Coloradans' love for their "purple mountain majesties," however. Outdoor activities such as skiing, mountain biking, and river rafting are popular. As for taking care of their beautiful state, thousands of Coloradans are involved in environmental protection projects.

The Faces of Colorado

Since its days as a U.S. territory, Colorado has been home to a population that is largely Caucasian, or white. People of Hispanic descent have always made up the largest ethnic minority. They outnumber all other minority groups combined. The same ratio, or proportion, holds true today. Caucasians make up almost 86 percent of the population. Some are direct descendants of European and American explorers and settlers who came to the region hundreds of years ago. Others are from families that have lived in Colorado for the last few decades. Colorado residents may also come from different parts of the country. A portion

Kids play in a Denver park. More than half of Colorado's population lives in the Denver-Boulder-Greeley area.

Today, American Indians make up about one percent of Colorado's population. This Ute woman works in a pottery factory.

of the Caucasian population in the state is of European descent. They may be from, or have family from, Great Britain, Scotland, Ireland, France, Germany, or Italy.

American Indians

The people with the longest history in Colorado are today one of its smallest minority groups. American Indians account for only about one percent of the population. More than 45,000 native peoples live in the state, which is also home to two Ute reservations. There are about 21,000 Indians from more than two hundred different tribes living in the Denver metro area alone. Unlike many other minorities, they do not live in a particular neighborhood. They live throughout the Denver metropolitan area. The Southern Ute Reservation is located in south-central Colorado. The Ute Mountain Reservation is farther west and spreads into the neighboring states of Utah and New Mexico.

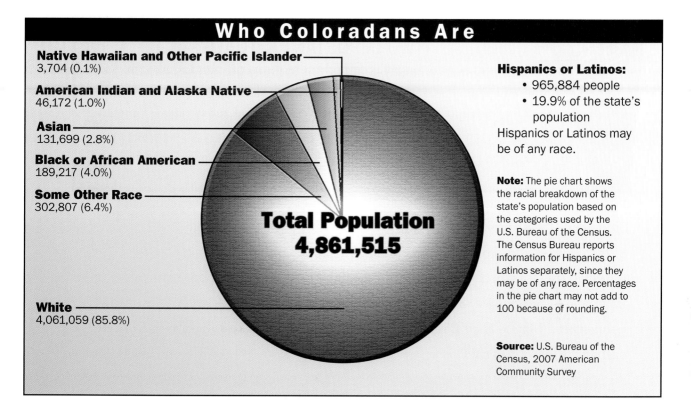

Who Coloradans Are

Native Hawaiian and Other Pacific Islander
3,704 (0.1%)

American Indian and Alaska Native
46,172 (1.0%)

Asian
131,699 (2.8%)

Black or African American
189,217 (4.0%)

Some Other Race
302,807 (6.4%)

White
4,061,059 (85.8%)

**Total Population
4,861,515**

Hispanics or Latinos:
- 965,884 people
- 19.9% of the state's population

Hispanics or Latinos may be of any race.

Note: The pie chart shows the racial breakdown of the state's population based on the categories used by the U.S. Bureau of the Census. The Census Bureau reports information for Hispanics or Latinos separately, since they may be of any race. Percentages in the pie chart may not add to 100 because of rounding.

Source: U.S. Bureau of the Census, 2007 American Community Survey

It can be a struggle for native peoples to live in the modern world while still trying to hold on to their ancient traditions. Organizations such as the Southern Ute Cultural Center can help. Through its museum, the group aims to be "the principal conservator and interpreter of our Tribe's history, our stories, our culture, and its artifacts." The Ute Mountain Tribal Park encompasses lands that contain native rock art and ancient dwellings. The Southern Utes also host a Bear Dance each spring, as well as a Sundance ceremony in the summer. The Bear Dance and the Sundance are both important ceremonies that have been practiced among the Utes for hundreds of years.

Still, in the hustle and bustle of modern life, the old ways can get lost. The Ute language has nearly disappeared. Only a handful of adults speak it, and the children are not learning it.

Teacher Stacey Oberly decided to do something about that. In 1999, she began teaching Ute to her kindergartners and first graders at a school on the

TWO IMPORTANT RITUALS

The Sundance ceremony is important to many different American Indian tribes. It is (and always has been) performed as a petition to the spirit world—to ensure the future prosperity of the people. Though the Bear Dance started as a Ute ritual, many other tribes also perform it. It is meant to celebrate the reawakening of life after the long winter.

Southern Ute Reservation. To make the learning fun, she held up flash cards of familiar objects, colors, and animals. The children would shout out the appropriate Ute word. Oberly knew that flash cards could not save the ancient language of her people. Still, for these five- and six-year-old students, it was a good start. "Maybe they'll remember a few words and take some pride in their culture," Oberly has said.

A Ute father and daughter share a smile. Today, only a few of Colorado's people speak the Ute language.

Colorado's lieutenant governor, Barbara O'Brien, takes part in a Bear Dance on a Ute reservation.

Famous Coloradans

Florence R. Sabin: Scientist

Florence R. Sabin was born in Central City in 1871. She graduated from Johns Hopkins Medical School in Maryland, and was the first woman to become a full professor at that school. Sabin spent years studying the human lymphatic system, cells, and blood vessels. She also did important medical research on tuberculosis. In the 1940s, she worked with the Colorado government to improve the state's health system. Sabin died in 1953.

Ruth Handler: Inventor

Ruth Handler, who was born in Denver in 1916, created a new kind of doll. Unlike the baby dolls that were popular at the time, her doll was a teenager, complete with makeup and high heels. Handler's Barbie doll first appeared in 1959 at a toy industry trade show and went on to become one of the best-selling toys of all time. Handler died in California in 2002.

M. Scott Carpenter: Astronaut

Scott Carpenter was born in Boulder in 1925. In 1962, he became the second astronaut to orbit Earth. Three years later, he went from space to the sea. He lived and worked on the ocean floor in the Navy's Sealab II project.

Ben Nighthorse Campbell: U.S. Senator

Colorado senator Ben Nighthorse Campbell is the son of a Portuguese immigrant mother and a Northern Cheyenne father. He was born in California in 1933 and moved to the Southern Ute Indian Reservation in 1977. In 1992, he became the first American Indian in sixty years to be seated in the U.S. Senate. He served in the Senate until 2005.

Tim Allen: Actor

Tim Allen, who was born in Denver in 1953, began his career as a standup comic. He went on to star in the hit television show *Home Improvement*. Today, he is a movie star, providing the voice of Buzz Lightyear in Disney's *Toy Story* films and starring in many other successful movies.

Amy Van Dyken: Olympic Swimmer

Amy Van Dyken, who was born in Englewood in 1973, suffered from severe asthma as a child. When Van Dyken was six, her doctor suggested she take up swimming to improve her condition. Then, in 1996, something incredible happened. Van Dyken became the first American woman to win four gold medals at one Olympic Games. That year, in Atlanta, Van Dyken won the 400 medley relay, the 400 freestyle relay, the 100 butterfly, and the 50 freestyle.

Second graders in Denver watch as President Barack Obama delivers a televised speech on September 8, 2009. Coloradans include people of many races and ethnic groups.

A Diverse Citizenry

According to 2007 population estimates from the U.S. Census Bureau, Hispanics accounted for almost 20 percent of Colorado's population. Hispanics are people whose families come from places such as Mexico, Central America, the Caribbean, South America, or Spain. The majority of Colorado's Hispanics in 2007, almost 690,000 people, were of Mexican descent

African Americans make up about 4 percent of the population, and almost 3 percent of Coloradans are of Asian descent. This includes Asian Indians, as well as people from China, Japan, Korea, Vietnam, and the Philippines.

Statewide percentages can be misleading, though. They show very little about how people actually live. Minorities are not scattered evenly across the state.

Some areas have almost no minority population. Other areas have thriving communities of one or more minority groups.

In Colorado, a variety of programs and organizations are available to help newcomers from foreign nations. Immigrants can find everything from medical and mental health services to English

Children from an elementary school in Littleton reenact a Civil War battle in Chatfield State Park.

Education is an important issue for many Colorado residents. These kids are in pottery class.

classes, job training, and legal aid. Schools offer special programs for immigrant students and their families. For example, school districts are hiring bilingual and multilingual staff members to help parents with questions about their children's education. They are setting up multicultural education programs in schools with large numbers of immigrant children.

Education: A Colorado Issue

Regardless of where they come from or how long they have been living in the state, many Colorado residents see education as an important issue. During local

Fourth-grade students display social-studies projects about Colorado history.

Bilingual education is a controversial topic in many Colorado schools.

and state elections, citizens often take the politicians' views on education into account when voting. During votes for town or city budgets, many voters are often in favor of giving large amounts of money to the public school systems. Coloradans want to ensure that the public schools are able to offer young residents a high level of education, enough teachers, and enough resources.

Bilingual education has become a controversial topic in Colorado schools. The idea behind bilingual education seems simple, but there are many viewpoints. Bilingual education would allow students who do not speak English to study subjects such as history and science in their native language.

Supporters of bilingual education believe that this is the best option because students would not fall behind in their studies while they are learning English. Opponents believe that bilingual education slows down students' progress in English. They argue that some students would not learn English at all, but continue to rely on their native language. The additional expense of hiring bilingual educators is also a concern. Some people believe that the money should be used for resources that all students in the schools could use.

The bilingual education debate is over methods, not goals. Both sides agree that English fluency is important. Without it, students have a difficult time attending college and finding jobs. Opponents of bilingual education proposed new laws that would nearly eliminate it in Colorado schools. The most recent anti-bilingual laws were defeated. But this issue will continue to affect the state.

Quick Facts

TRAGEDY AT COLUMBINE

On April 20, 1999, Eric Harris and Dylan Klebold, seniors at Columbine High School in Denver, set off homemade bombs and opened fire on their teachers and classmates with handguns, a rifle, and a shotgun. Ultimately, the boys killed thirteen people and injured twenty-three others before killing themselves. It was the deadliest high school shooting in American history, and most of it was played out on live TV.

Calendar of Events

★ Cinco de Mayo

Cinco de Mayo celebrates a Mexican victory over French invasion forces on May 5, 1862. Denver's Cinco de Mayo celebration began as a small street fair in a Mexican-American neighborhood. Today, it draws half a million people from all ethnic backgrounds. They flock to Civic Center Park to enjoy traditional Mexican music, food, and arts and crafts.

★ Aspen Music Festival

Every summer, classical music enthusiasts attend the nine-week Aspen Music Festival. They gather under an enormous tent that gives the concerts a "music under the stars" flavor. The 350 events include concerts, classes, lectures, and even kids' programs.

★ Greeley Independence Stampede

The Greeley Independence Stampede bills itself as the World's Largest 4th of July Rodeo & Western Celebration. The rodeo itself is the centerpiece of a celebration that lasts two weeks. It features country music concerts, a carnival midway, and many "down-home" events like a flapjack feed and a watermelon feast.

★ Dragon Boat Festival

Every summer, Chinese dragon boat races bring thousands of people to Sloan's Lake Park in Denver. The boats, with their bright dragon's heads and tails, hold up to twenty rowers, who time their strokes to the beating of a drum. In addition to the races, the event features an Asian marketplace and performances ranging from Chinese lion dancing to Japanese taiko drumming.

★ Leadville Boom Days

Every August, people gather in Leadville to celebrate the state's Old West history. Activities at this festival include mining contests, a motorcycle rodeo, burro races, music, and craft and food booths.

★ Colorado State Fair

Colorado's state fair is held in Pueblo every August. Residents and visitors watch and participate in a rodeo, races, parades, games, and concerts. The fair also hosts a fine arts show, livestock exhibitions, and cultural events.

★ Arkansas Valley Balloon Festival

The first weekend in November is hot-air ballooning time in the small southeastern Colorado town of Rocky Ford. The autumn sky is alive with soaring balloons in many colors, as ballooning enthusiasts and spectators gather for three days of festivities. With plenty of food and activities for the whole family, spectators have as much fun as the balloonists.

★ Rocky Mountain Country Christmas

Colorado City's Christmas celebration begins in late November. Every weekend until Christmas, the downtown area steps back in time one hundred years. You may see horse-drawn carriages in the streets and costumed carolers on the sidewalks.

How the Government Works

Colorado's constitution was adopted in 1876, when Colorado became a state. Though the constitution has been amended, or changed, over the years, it has never been replaced. Like the U.S. Constitution, Colorado's constitution describes the duties of the state government's three branches: the executive, the legislative, and the judicial. It remains the foundation for Colorado's entire system of government.

Levels of Government

Colorado's government begins at the local level, with towns, cities, and counties. The governing body of a town is called a board of trustees. The governing body of a city is called a council. Municipal (city and town) governments make ordinances (local laws), covering a variety of local concerns. For example, municipal governments can regulate traffic and parking on city streets. They can also separate business areas from residential areas with zoning ordinances. Cities and larger towns have municipal courts to deal with minor crimes and violations of local laws.

Cities and towns are part of counties. Colorado's sixty-four counties are responsible for carrying out state programs on a local level. Counties are governed by a board of elected commissioners. Other offices within the county include tax assessor, treasurer, and sheriff.

Elected officials meet at Colorado's State Capitol in Denver.

Branches of Government

EXECUTIVE ★

The executive branch consists of the governor, lieutenant governor, and different departments that cover various aspects of public life. The secretary of state, attorney general, and treasurer, as well as the governor and lieutenant governor, are elected by voters. Other department heads are appointed by the governor, with the approval of the state senate. Elected officials in the executive branch serve four-year terms. They cannot serve more than two consecutive terms.

LEGISLATIVE ★

Colorado's legislature, or lawmaking body, is called the general assembly. It is made up of two houses. The senate has thirty-six members, and the house of representatives has sixty-five members. Members of the senate serve four-year terms and cannot hold office for more than two consecutive terms. Members of the house of representatives serve two-year terms and may be elected for up to four consecutive terms. Any proposed law must be passed by a majority vote in both houses of the legislature before it goes to the governor for executive approval.

JUDICIAL ★

The judicial branch enforces the laws of the state. Colorado's court system ranges from municipal (city) and county courts up to the state supreme court. State judges are not elected. They are appointed by the governor. However, during general elections, voters get to decide whether or not to retain the judges. District court judges appear on the ballot every six years. Appeals judges are up for approval every eight years, and supreme court judges are up every ten years.

Home Rule

In Colorado, local governments can elect to have home rule, which gives them more control over local matters. Home rule communities can tailor government policies to their particular needs. They can create their own budget guidelines and zoning regulations. Colorado has close to one hundred cities and towns that are home rule municipalities. The largest is Colorado Springs.

Federal and statewide laws still apply, which places some practical limits on what home rule communities can do. For example, home rule communities must budget for state-mandated (that is, state-ordered) programs before they fund their own projects.

Lieutenant governor Barbara O'Brien has the authority to sign bills into law when the governor is out of state.

Contacting Lawmakers

★ ★ ★ ★ ★ ★ ★ ★ ★ ★ ★ ★

If you are interested in learning about Colorado's legislators, you can go to this website:

http://www.leg.state.co.us

There, you will find information about current legislation and contact information for state senators and representatives.

How a Bill Becomes a Law

Sometimes a state resident, official, or legislator comes up with an idea for a new state law. The idea is then passed on to a member of the general assembly. The reason is that only a state senator or state representative can officially introduce proposals for new laws. The proposed law is a written document called a bill. A bill can be introduced in either house. The bill is given a number and placed on the schedule of the house that will consider it first. On the appointed day, the bill's sponsor introduces it on the floor.

After this first reading, the bill is assigned to a committee for complete review. Which committee is assigned to analyze a bill depends upon the topic of that bill. For example, a senate bill about water conservation would go to the Committee on Agriculture and Natural Resources. A house bill on the same topic would go to the Committee on Agriculture, Livestock, and Natural Resources.

After studying the bill, the committee may postpone it, amend certain parts, or recommend it for passage. Unless a bill is postponed, it will go back to the floor for a second reading. The entire senate or house discusses, debates, and proposes additional amendments to the bill. After this process, they vote. The bill may be accepted as amended, rejected, held over to another day, or sent back to the committee for additional work.

Bills that pass the committee process go on to a yet another reading. After this third reading, there is a final vote. If a bill passes the final vote, it is introduced to the second house, where the whole process is repeated.

Even when a bill is passed by both houses, the legislators' task may not be done. It often happens that the house and senate adopt different versions of the bill. In these cases, the differences must be fixed before a final version of the bill goes to the governor for his or her signature.

The governor can accept or reject the bill. If the governor signs the bill, it becomes law. If the governor vetoes—or rejects—the bill, it can still pass as long as three-fourths of both houses vote for the law.

Colorado author T. A. Barron founded the Gloria Barron Prize for Young Heroes.

Making a Difference

Coloradans are known for taking an active interest in government and social issues. People of all ages become involved in many ways. To honor young people who make a difference in their communities, Colorado children's author T. A. Barron founded the Gloria Barron Prize for Young Heroes. Every year, ten outstanding achievers are recognized—five for their efforts on behalf of their communities and fellow beings, and five for their efforts on behalf of the environment. In 2001, the first year the awards were given out, they went to ten kids from Colorado. The next year, the judging was expanded to include kids from all over the country. Coloradans continue to make the cut. Past winners include a twelve-year-old Boulder girl who organized Showers to Go. This program gave free personal-care kits to homeless people. A thirteen-year-old girl from Evergreen founded an organization that provides education, food, and clothing to girls in a Peruvian orphanage. A thirteen-year-old Denver boy organized a bowl-a-thon that raised $9,000 to help a young burn-victim's family with its medical bills.

These students knew their projects would not solve the problem of health-care costs or homelessness. But they saw a need and found a way to help.

Making a Living

For many years, agriculture and mining were the mainstays of Colorado's economy. That began to change in the mid–twentieth century as technology and service industries grew in importance. The service industry includes business, professional, medical, and consumer services. Manufacturing and transportation continue to be important, and tourism has grown along with the service and technology industries.

Colorado's New Economy

Agriculture, mining, and manufacturing are part of what is sometimes called the Old Economy. This economy was created by the farm, the mine, and the factory. The New Economy is created by computers, the Internet, and other new technologies.

These new technologies will not replace Colorado's Old Economy; they will coexist with it. In fact, technology benefits the Old Economy in many ways. Technology can make operations more efficient and less costly. For example, farmers in eastern Colorado can now computerize their business records, track crop prices and weather systems online, and carry cell phones out to the farthest reaches of their property. Farmers can also use advanced computer systems to map their fields and track the success of crops and irrigation techniques.

Tourism is an important part of Colorado's economy.
Many people come to enjoy the state's natural beauty.

Agriculture

Colorado's four leading crops are corn, wheat, hay, and potatoes. These crops account for 90 percent of the total value from all field crops in the state, with the exception of sugar beets. In 2007, these crops were valued at $2 billion.

Some enterprising farmers in Colorado have turned their cornfields into tourist attractions. One of these farmers, Bill English, created a large maze by planting 11 acres (4 hectares) of corn in the shape of the Colorado state seal. Hundreds of visitors paid admission to try their luck at navigating the twists and turns of this designer cornfield. Other farmers have created corn mazes in different designs for family fun.

This Colorado cornfield has been made into a maze. Corn is one of the state's most important crops.

RECIPE FOR PEACH COBBLER

Western Colorado has a good climate for growing peaches. Here is a recipe that is perfect for this sweet fruit.

WHAT YOU NEED

5 cups (900 grams) fresh sliced peaches

1 $\frac{1}{4}$ cup (335 g) sugar

Cinnamon

Nutmeg

1 cup (110 g) self-rising flour

1 large egg

$\frac{1}{2}$ cup (115 g) butter or margarine

Place the sliced peaches in a large bowl and sprinkle ¼ cup (50 g) of the sugar on the slices. Add a little bit of cinnamon and nutmeg. Gently move the peaches around so that the slices are lightly coated with the sugar and spices. Pour the coated peach slices into a shallow baking dish.

In another bowl combine the rest of the sugar and flour. Beat the egg and add it to the flour and sugar mixture. This mixture should be crumbly. Pour it over the peaches. Melt the butter and pour it over the topping.

Have an adult help you with the oven. Bake the cobbler for 30 minutes at 350 °F (180 °C), or until the topping turns slightly brown and crusty.

You can serve this dish warm or cold and add a scoop of your favorite ice cream.

FARM COUNTRY
Colorado has more than
30,000 farms and ranches
across the state, encompassing
almost 31 million acres
(12.5 million hectares). That is
equal to almost half the state's
total land area.

In western Colorado around Grand Junction, farmers grow wine grapes and tree fruits such as apples, peaches, apricots, and cherries. These crops are sold throughout the state and to the rest of the country. Some of the produce is packaged or used in food-processing factories in the state.

In both eastern and western Colorado, raising livestock is actually more profitable than farming. In fact, 75 percent of the Colorado's agricultural production comes from livestock and livestock products, such as corn for feed. The raising of cattle and calves provides more than 60 percent of the state's agricultural revenue.

Another profitable area for farmers is specialty crops. Small farmers in particular have found that crops such as herbs, ornamental plants, and sod for lawns earn more than traditional field crops such as wheat and corn.

Mining

The days of "Pikes Peak or Bust" are long gone. But mining remains an important industry in Colorado. Coal is an important mineral to Colorado, which ranks eighth among U.S. states in coal production. In 2008, 32 million tons (29 million metric tons) of coal were mined in the state, with a value of $887 million.

Colorado mines produce millions of tons of other minerals, including gypsum, limestone, molybdenum, titanium, and uranium. Molybdenum is used as an alloy in stainless steel. It makes the steel tougher, harder, and more able to resist corrosion. Colorado is the leading producer of this metal in the United States. Colorado is also a leader in the production of triuranium octoxide (U_3O_8), a stable form of uranium. In 2008, the state produced a total of 407,000 pounds (185,000 kg) of U_3O_8. Gunnison County, Colorado, is also home to the largest reserves of titanium in the United States.

Although Colorado is no longer experiencing a gold rush, the state still ranks fourth in the country (behind Nevada, Alaska, and Utah) in gold production. In 2008, the Cripple Creek and Victor Mine produced almost 260,000 troy ounces (8,000 kg) of this precious metal.

Manufacturing

Manufacturing is the process of taking raw materials (such as cotton) and adding value to them by turning them into finished products (such as cloth). Products

Colorado ranks fourth in the United States for gold production.

A research technician prepares a wind turbine gearbox for testing. Wind energy is a "clean" energy source.

manufactured in Colorado include scientific instruments, such as medical devices and electronic equipment, as well as machinery, such as computers and communications equipment. The state also has a large food processing manufacturing industry. This includes meatpacking, production of animal feed, and beer brewing. The Coors Brewing Company in Golden, Colorado, has been in operation since 1873. The company employs thousands of people and produces billions of barrels of beer every year.

Colorado is also leading the county in "green" manufacturing. In March 2008, Danish energy company Vestas opened—in Windsor, Colorado—the first U.S. factory to manufacture blades for wind turbines. These modern-day windmills are used to generate electricity. Wind energy—a "clean" energy source—is one of the fastest-growing energy sources in the world today.

In 2009, Vestas broke ground on two new factories in Brighton—another blade facility and a nacelle assembly plant. (The nacelle is mounted on the top of the turbine and houses parts including the gearbox, generator, controller, and brake.) The plants were expected to be fully functioning in 2010 and to employ about 1,350 people between them. Vestas is also building a plant in Pueblo to manufacture the towers for wind turbines. The company says the factory will be the largest of its kind in the world.

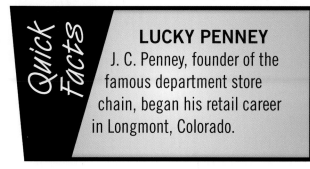

Wholesale and Retail Trade

Wholesalers are the link between manufacturers who make the merchandise and retailers who sell to the general public. Wholesalers buy from manufacturers in large quantities and then sell smaller quantities to retailers, who in turn sell the products to consumers. About 3.2 percent of Colorado's workforce is employed in wholesale trade, while 11.4 percent work in retail.

The retail industry includes everything from restaurants and bars to supermarkets, department stores, and specialty shops. In addition to day-to-day retail establishments, such as gas stations, supermarkets, and pharmacies, Denver and other cities have major centers that transform shopping into a recreational activity.

For example, Denver's Cherry Creek neighborhood has tree-lined streets with more than 420 businesses, including department stores, specialty shops, art galleries, and restaurants. Locals and tourists alike enjoy spending time at Cherry Creek, browsing in shops or eating in the restaurants. Businesses like these help the economy in a few ways. The stores provide a place to sell products manufactured in Colorado. The jobs created by these stores and restaurants keep many Coloradans employed. The taxes that consumers pay when purchasing from these businesses go back to the state.

Products & Resources

Coal

Colorado coal is taken from the western stretches of the state. It is burned for heating and generating electricity. It supplies about 72 percent of Colorado's electricity.

Field Crops

The largest crops in Colorado include corn, wheat, hay, and potatoes. The hay, and some of the corn, is used to feed livestock in the state and is also sent to other parts of the country.

Ski Resorts

Colorado's resorts are perfect for skiing, snowboarding, or snowmobiling. The ski industry alone accounts for nearly $2 billion of Colorado's income. Every year more than 11 million people come to Colorado to ski and snowboard.

Cattle

Colorado cattle and calves account for more than 60 percent of the state's agricultural products. The beef is sold within the state, across the country, and around the world. Colorado ranchers export beef to places such as Japan, the United Kingdom, and Canada.

Office Equipment

Some Colorado factories make office products such as computers and other electronics. These products are used in offices across the state and around the country. Research companies based in the state use new technologies to develop new machines and products.

Greenhouses and Nurseries

Besides growing crops to feed people and animals, Colorado farms are used to grow plants and flowers. Greenhouses and nurseries across the state grow small trees, flowers, and shrubs that are sent to florists in the state and around the country. Many greenhouses are also used for plant research.

Tourism adds almost $10 billion a year to Colorado's economy. Many visitors enjoy strolling and shopping along Pearl Street in Boulder.

Service Industries

A service is an activity or process that one person performs for another. It does not transfer ownership of any physical object. A business that rents cars is a service, while one that sells them is not.

Service industries include everything from banking and insurance to health care, education, transportation, and communications. In addition to these, thousands of providers offer personal and domestic services such as hair styling, child care, and home improvement.

Technology has created many new service jobs. For example, many Coloradans are making a living by programming computers, designing Web pages, installing digital television cable, or performing other technical services.

In 1999, Colorado's general assembly created a new agency: the Governor's Office of Innovation and Technology (OIT). The mission of this office is to attract high-technology industries to the state, develop training programs to expand the technology workforce, and create a high-speed fiber optic network to streamline government operations. In 2009, the OIT released a report that identified ways to make the state's health care system more efficient and effective. According to the report, new information technology will modernize Colorado's health-care system and make higher quality, more affordable health care available to residents.

Tourism and Recreational Services

Colorado has a thriving tourist industry. There are 200,000 people working in the tourism industry, which makes it the largest employer in the state. Altogether, tourism adds almost $10 billion a year to the Colorado economy.

In winter, people come from all over the world to the state's ski resorts. In summer, they come for camping, river rafting, rock climbing, and many other outdoor activities.

Every year about 4 million people visit Colorado's four national parks: Rocky Mountain, Mesa Verde, Great Sand Dunes, and Black Canyon of the Gunnison. There, they can experience some of the most incredible natural and cultural wonders the country has to offer, including the highest sand dunes in North America, one of the deepest canyons in the Western Hemisphere, and, of course, the magnificent cliff dwellings of the Ancestral Pueblo people. The state also has forty-one state parks, which provide amazing opportunities for outdoor recreation and adventure.

Many people also visit Colorado for its professional sports teams. The Denver Nuggets are the state's NBA team. Invesco Field at Mile High is home to the Denver Broncos football team. NHL fans attend the games played by the state's hockey team, the Colorado Avalanche. The Colorado Rockies are the state's Major League Baseball team. Denver is the smallest metropolitan area in the United States to have professional teams in all four sports. The state's economy benefits from the money spent on game tickets and souvenirs.

Taking Care of Colorado

Environmental protection has long been an important issue for Coloradans. There are laws and programs to preserve open spaces, protect endangered wildlife, and develop clean sources of energy. A group called the Colorado Renewable Energy Society (CRES) develops plans to help conserve energy and use renewable resources such as wind and solar power.

Colorado already leads the nation in wind-energy production. As of 2009, the state had eight wind farms that provided 1,060 megawatts of electricity. That is enough to power about 850,000 homes. In 2009, Duke Energy Corporation announced plans to build a ninth—$100 million—wind farm on the eastern Colorado plains. The thirty-four-turbine farm will be built on 6,000 acres (2,400 ha) near Burlington and will generate fifty-one megawatts of electricity.

One of the state's most difficult resource management problems is also one of the oldest: water. In this semiarid state, there never seems to be enough of it, and the distribution is uneven. Most of the state's water comes from the mountains.

Workers & Industries

Industry	Number of People Working in That Industry	Percentage of All Workers Who Are Working in That Industry
Education and health care	433,383	17.9%
Wholesale and retail businesses	353,776	14.6%
Publishing, media, entertainment, hotels, and restaurants	326,919	13.4%
Professionals, scientists, and managers	303,458	12.5%
Construction	234,358	9.7%
Banking and finance, insurance, and real estate	194,088	8.0%
Manufacturing	180,124	7.4%
Other services	122,980	5.1%
Transportation and public utilities	116,024	4.8%
Government	108,403	4.5%
Farming, fishing, forestry, and mining	51,021	2.1%
Totals	**2,424,534**	**100%**

Notes: Figures above do not include people in the armed forces. "Professionals" includes people such as doctors and lawyers. Percentages may not add to 100 because of rounding.

Source: U.S. Bureau of the Census, 2007 estimates

The state's annual precipitation is generally less than 20 inches (50 cm), with the driest areas receiving only 10 inches (25 cm). In the mountains, the highest elevations may receive as much as 50 inches (125 cm) per year.

Colorado has an advanced system of dams, tunnels, and reservoirs to distribute and conserve water resources. Even with all the planning and technology, droughts are a constant danger. In very dry years, Coloradans may face mandatory water rationing.

Looking Forward

Coloradans are aware that the unique beauty of their state is an economic asset. It is the foundation for their high quality of life, and the reason that millions of people visit the state each year. Preserving the beauty of the landscape while continuing to develop a variety of industries will be Colorado's challenge for the twenty-first century.

State Flag & Seal

Colorado's state flag was adopted in 1911. It has two blue stripes and one white stripe. The flag features a large red C surrounding a golden disk.

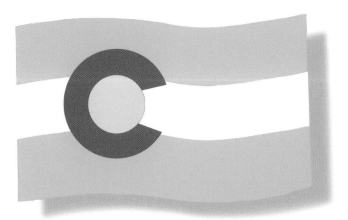

Colorado's state seal features a shield with three snow-capped mountains and mining tools. Below the shield is the state motto in Latin, which translates to "Nothing Without the Deity." A pyramid with the eye of God and a bundle of wooden rods with an ax are located above the shield. The bundle of rods represents the strength lacking in a single rod; the ax symbolizes authority and leadership. Colorado's year of statehood, 1876, is displayed at the bottom of the seal.

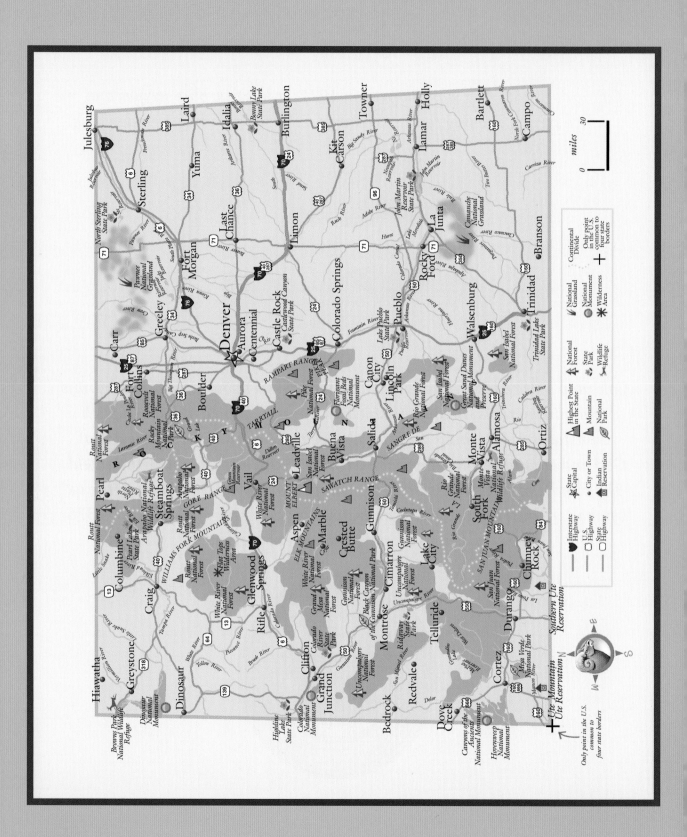

State Song

Where the Columbines Grow

words and music by Arthur John Fynn

BOOKS

Gonzales, Doreen. *Rocky Mountain National Park: Adventure, Explore, Discover*. Berkeley Heights, NJ: Enslow, 2009.

Perry, Phyllis J. *A Kid's Look at Colorado*. Golden, CO: Fulcrum Publishing, 2005.

Quigley, Mary. *Mesa Verde*. Chicago, IL: Heinemann-Raintree, 2005.

Shirley, Gayle C. *Amazing Animals of Colorado*. Guilford, CT: Globe Pequot Press, 2005.

WEBSITES

Colorado State Parks:
www.parks.state.co.us

The Official Colorado State Website:
www.colorado.gov

The Official Site for Colorado Travel and Tourism:
www.colorado.com

Linda Jacobs Altman has written many books for young people. She and her husband live in a small California town near a lake, with a house full of dogs, cats, and birds.

Stephanie Fitzgerald has been writing nonfiction for children for more than ten years, and she is the author of more than twenty books. Her specialties include history, wildlife, and popular culture. Stephanie lives in Stamford, Connecticut, with her husband and their daughter.

Page numbers in **boldface** are illustrations.